NnOoPp
QqRr
SsTtUu
VvWw
XxYyZz

volume **1**

BIG BIRD'S
SESAME STREET®
DICTIONARY

FEATURING JIM HENSON'S SESAME STREET MUPPETS

LETTERS A–B

by Linda Hayward
illustrated by Joe Mathieu
Editor in Chief: Sharon Lerner

Art Directors: Grace Clarke and Cathy Goldsmith
with special thanks to Judith M. Leary

Funk & Wagnalls, Inc./Children's Television Workshop

Since 1969 the *Sesame Street* television show has made learning an enjoyable and natural part of daily life for millions of children. *The Sesame Street Dictionary* fosters the same important educational goals. It is more than a standard beginner's dictionary, and many unique features make these volumes books with which a child can *grow* from age three to age eight. They have been carefully designed to be used in three stages:

- as word books and vocabulary builders,
- as reading-readiness storybooks,
- as a first dictionary.

A primary goal of *The Sesame Street Dictionary* is to make using a dictionary an enjoyable as well as a rewarding experience. The exciting and humorous visual presentation invites the exploration of words and helps establish at an early age a positive attitude toward using dictionaries. Long before a child is old enough to read, he or she can *see* that this dictionary is fun. At the same time, *The Sesame Street Dictionary* provides accurate, complete, and easily understood information. More than 1,300 words are defined, illustrated, and used in context in one or more sample sentences.

The definitions are short, straightforward, and unusually clear and accurate. The vocabulary is structured for beginning readers. In all cases the definitions reflect the primary meaning of the word in terms of a child's world.

The word selection was based on several current vocabulary lists compiled by well-known educators. The dictionary concentrates on words that appear frequently in beginning reading books and in a young child's everyday world. Other words, such as *rocket, dinosaur,* and *skeleton,* were chosen because they fascinate children.

The lively, colorful illustrations reinforce and in many cases expand the definition of the word. For example, the verb *blow* is illustrated with four pictures in which a Muppet first blows *on* a trombone, then blows *up* a balloon, blows *away* bubbles, and finally blows *out* a birthday candle. This comic-strip-style flexibility gives the dictionary an exciting storybook appearance.

Games, riddles, and jokes are another unique feature of these books. These activities are used not only to reinforce word meanings but also to present educational concepts such as naming the parts of the body, counting, sorting objects by their characteristics, measuring, and relationships.

The skillful integration of text and visual presentation results in a dictionary that is totally different from all other beginning dictionaries. Whether used as a word book with three- and four-year-olds, as a storybook with five- and six-year-olds, or as a useful dictionary with beginning readers, *The Sesame Street Dictionary* makes learning fun.

—*Sharon Lerner,*
Editor in Chief

Aa

A B C D E F G H I J K L M N O P Q R S T U V W X Y Z

a A is a word that means one.

Bert is reaching for **a** book.

able When you are able to do something, you can do it.

Bert is **able** to reach the book. Ernie is not **able** to reach that high.

about About means on the subject of.

> I wonder what this dictionary says **about** pigeons.

A dictionary is a book **about** words.

about About can also mean a little more or a little less or almost.

> There are **about** thirteen hundred words in this dictionary.

above When you are above something, you are higher than it is.

> Hello, everybod-ee! I, Grover, am flying my little airplane **above** the trees.

> Uh-oh! Now I am *not* **above** the trees.

accident An accident is something that happens by mistake.

> Oops! Your old pal Grover had a little **accident**.

across   When you go across something, you move from one side to the other side.

Cookie Monster, tell me a monster riddle.

Sure, Betty Lou.... Why did the monster go **across** Sesame Street?

To get to the other side!

act   When you act, you pretend to be someone or something else.

Oh, boy! I get to **act** the part of Jack.

SESAME STREET PLAYERS IN JACK AND THE BEANSTALK

actor   An actor is someone who acts.

Why do I always have to be the beanstalk?

SESAME STREET PLAYERS IN JACK AND THE BEANSTALK

Ernie and Bert are **actors.** They are acting in a play. The audience is watching them.

add   When you add to something, you make it bigger.

I am going to **add** one more block to my tower.

add   When you add numbers or things, you find out how many there are all together.

$\begin{array}{r} 2 \\ +1 \\ \hline 3 \end{array}$

If I **add** two apples and one apple, I get three apples.

address   Your address is where you live.

ERNIE AND BERT 123 SESAME ST.

U.S. MAIL

Ernie and Bert live at 123 Sesame Street. 123 Sesame Street is their **address.**

adult An adult is someone who has grown up.

> Our father, mother, and grandmother are the **adults** in our house.

> My brother and I are the children.

adventure An adventure is something exciting that happens to someone.

> Mommy, will you please read me the **adventures** of Super Grover?

afraid When you feel afraid, you are scared or frightened.

> Don't be **afraid,** dear. Mommy is here.

Grover is **afraid** of the dark.

after After means later than.

> Greetings! I am the Count! Do you know what I am doing? I am brushing my teeth.

> And **after** I brush my teeth, I count them. One clean tooth, two clean teeth…

afternoon Afternoon is the time of the day that comes between morning and night.

> Time for my **afternoon** snack!

again When you do something again, you do it one more time.

> I'm Rodeo Rosie. And when I fall off a bucking bronco…

> I get right back on **again!**

against   Against means upon or touching.

against   Against can also mean on opposite sides.

The Red Monster team is playing **against** the Blue Monster team.

age   Your age is how old you are.

The Busby twins are the same **age.**

agree   When people agree, they think the same way or want the same things.

The Busby twins **agree** about striped shirts.

ahead   When you are ahead, you are in front.

The tortoise and the hare are having a race. The hare is **ahead.**

air   Air is what you breathe. Air is all around you. It is what you feel when the wind blows.

airplane An airplane is something that you ride in. An airplane has wings and can move through the sky.

airport An airport is a place where airplanes take off and land.

Grover is landing his **airplane** at the **airport.**

alarm An alarm is a buzzer or a bell that wakes you or warns you.

The **alarm** on Big Bird's clock wakes him up.

The fire **alarm** warns the fire fighters that there is a fire.

alike When things are alike, they are the same.

The Busby twins look **alike.**

alive Things that are alive need food and water.

Plants are **alive.**

Animals are **alive.**

People are **alive.**

Rocks are not **alive.**

all   All means everything with nothing left over.

Gee, Bert, I don't know. I guess you have **all** the luck.

Ernie, why am I carrying **all** the groceries?

alligator   An alligator is an animal with lots of teeth and a long tail.

Hi! My name is Prairie Dawn. I wonder why most people are afraid of **alligators.**

Oh!

allow   When you allow people to do something, you let them do it.

It has come to my attention that some of you are smiling. Well, smiling is not **allowed.** If you promise not to smile, I will **allow** you to read this dictionary.

almost   Almost means nearly.

The cookies are **almost** gone.

alone   When you are alone, no one is with you.

Hello again! Remember me? I am the Count and I love to count things. When I am **alone,** I count myself. 1…one Count!

along   When you go along something, you move from one end toward the other end.

Sherlock Hemlock is walking **along** Sesame Street.

along   Along can also mean together with.

Ernie took Rubber Duckie **along** with him.

aloud Aloud means loud enough to be heard, not in a whisper.

Big Bird likes to read **aloud.**

> ABCDEFG…
> HIJKLMNOP…
> QRS…TUV…
> WXYZ.

ALPHABET BOOK

alphabet The alphabet is all the letters from A to Z.

> I, Sherlock Hemlock, the world's greatest detective, have discovered the world's longest word.

> Oh, Sherlock! That's not a word. It's the **alphabet.**

> Another way of saying **alphabet** is ABCs.

already Already means before now.

The Count is going to bed. He has **already** brushed his teeth.

also Also means too.

abcdefghijklmno
pqrstuvwxyz

> Hi! I'm Roosevelt Franklin. I know my letters from A to Z. I **also** know my numbers from 1 to 20.

1 2 3 4 5 6 7 8 9 10
11 12 13 14 15 16 17 18 19 20

always Always means all the time or every time.

Cookie Monster has a big appetite. He is **always** hungry.

Ernie **always** has Rubber Duckie with him when he takes a bath.

am Do you want to play WHO **AM** I?

I **am** Guy Smiley, star of daytime TV, here to play everybody's favorite game—WHO **AM** I?

I love to eat birdseed. Who **am** I?

I love to count birdseed. Who **am** I?

I love to find birdseed. Who **am** I?

I hate birdseed and I hate games. That is why I **am** hiding in my trash can.

WHO AM I?

among Among means in with or in the middle of.

Bert likes to walk **among** the pigeons.

among Among can also mean with some for each.

How do you divide four apples **among** five monsters?

You make applesauce.

amount Amount means how much or how many.

Now each one of us has the same **amount** of applesauce.

an An means one.

Grover is eating **an** apple.

and And means together with or also.

What is cute **and** lovable **and** blue **and** furry **and** goes up **and** down?

Grover the elevator operator!

angry When you get mad, you feel angry.

Ernie, please pick up these toys right away! This place is a mess!

Bert is **angry.**

animal An animal is any living thing that is not a plant. An animal can move from one place to another by itself. Most plants cannot.

Farmer Grover is feeding the **animals** on his farm.

another Another means one more.

I am picking a flower.

I am picking **another** flower. Now I have two flowers.

answer An answer is what you say to a question.

How much is one plus one?

The **answer** is two.

answer When you answer, you say something back.

Grover!

Yes, Mommy! I am coming!

When Grover's mother calls, Grover always **answers.**

ant An ant is a small, crawling insect.

Look! The **ants** are taking my picnic lunch! Am I angry? No, I am happy. Now I can count them. 1, 2, 3, 4, 5… five wonderful **ants!**

any Any means one or some.

We grouches don't like **any**body or **any**one or **any**thing. Turn the page so I will not have to look at you **any**more.

apartment An apartment is a place to live in. There are many apartments in an apartment building.

Bert is playing the accordion in his **apartment.**

appear When something appears, you can see it.

I, the Amazing Mumford, will wave my magic wand and a rabbit will **appear.**

A LA PEANUT BUTTER SANDWICHES!

Now where is that rabbit?

apple An apple is a fruit that grows on an apple tree.

Here is my favorite thing that begins with A—**apple.**

And here is *my* favorite thing that begins with A—**apple** core.

are Big Bird and Snuffle-upagus **are** best friends.

You **are** my best friend, Mr. Snuffle-upagus.

You **are** *my* best friend, Bird.

arm Your arm is the part of your body between your shoulder and your hand. Look up the word body.

around Around means in a circle.

Marshal Grover has a belt **around** his waist.

I have turned **around.** You cannot see my face.

artist   An artist is someone who makes or does special things.

Some **artists** make pictures.

Some **artists** make statues.

Some **artists** dance.

Some **artists** play musical instruments.

as   As means equal to.

Big Bird is **as** tall **as** eight big blocks.

ask   You ask a question when you want to find out the answer.

A detective has to **ask** many questions.

Who? What? Where? When? How? Why?

asleep   When you are asleep, you are not awake.

I wonder if Bert is **asleep**.... Oh, Bert. Are you **asleep**?

He doesn't hear me. I'll have to speak louder. HEY, BERT! ARE YOU **ASLEEP**?

No, Ernie. You woke me up. I *was* **asleep**. Now I am awake.

astronaut   An astronaut is someone who travels in a spaceship.

One small step for Grover Monster— one giant step for Monsterkind!

Grover the **astronaut** is on the moon.

at At tells when or where.

At night Little Bird likes to stay **at** home.

attention When you pay attention, you look and listen.

Herry Monster is not paying **attention**. He is bumping into everything.

aunt Your aunt is the sister of your mother or father.

AUNT ELMA

FATHER

Aunt Sally is my mother's sister. **Aunt** Elma is my father's sister.

AUNT SALLY

MOTHER

ME

author An author is someone who writes stories, poems, or plays.

Big Bird is the **author** of *Birds of a Feather*.

Birds of a Feather

autumn Autumn is the name of a season. Autumn comes after summer. Another name for autumn is fall.

It must be **autumn**. The leaves are turning red and yellow.

awake When you are awake, you are not sleeping.

Bert is still **awake**.

away Away means somewhere else.

At last! This is the end of the A words. Now you can go **away** and leave me alone.

Find the Things That Begin with the Letter **A**

Bb

A B C D E F G H I J K L M N O P Q R S T U V W X Y Z

baby   A baby is a very young child.

What do monsters have that nobody else has?

Baby monsters!

back   Your back is the part of your body opposite your chest and between your neck and your hips. Look up the word body.

Prairie Dawn is hiking. She has a pack on her **back**.

back   The back is also the part of a thing that is behind the front.

Grover's airplane has a propeller in front and a tail in **back**.

bad   When something is bad, it is not good.

This is a **bad** day for a picnic.

When you feel bad, you don't feel good.

Bert has caught a cold. He feels **bad**.

Ernie is sorry that Bert is sick. Ernie feels **bad**.

bag A bag is a kind of container. You can put things in a bag.

WHAT'S MY BAG?

Hi! I'm Guy Smiley, and it's time to play: WHAT'S MY **BAG**?

I carry the mail. What's my **bag**?

I sell groceries. What's my **bag**?

I collect trash. What's my **bag**?

GROCERY TRASH U.S. MAIL

bake When you bake something, you cook it in an oven.

baker A baker is someone who bakes.

bakery A bakery is the place where a baker bakes. A bakery is also a store where you can buy the things the baker bakes.

BAKERY

COOKIES

Everybody comes to Cookie's **bakery** to buy the cookies Cookie the **baker bakes.**

ball A ball is something to play with. Most balls are round.

Three of these things belong together. One of these things is not the same.

The baseball, the basketball, and the beach ball are all **balls**. The orange is a fruit, so it does not belong.

A foot**ball** is not round, but it is still called a **ball.**

balloon A balloon is a bag made of rubber. It can be filled with air or another kind of gas.

Prairie Dawn is blowing up a **balloon.**

banana A banana is a fruit that grows on banana trees.

Oh, Oscar! Here is my favorite thing that begins with the letter B—**banana.**

And here is my favorite thing that begins with the letter B—**banana** peel.

band A band is a group of people playing musical instruments together.

band A band is also a strip of material that goes around something.

bank A bank is a place or thing to keep money in.

bank A bank is also the high ground along the side of a river.

barber A barber is someone who cuts your hair.

Farley went to the **barber**shop. The **barber** cut Farley's hair.

bark A bark is a sound that a dog makes.

Barkley the dog can **bark** very loudly. The tree **bark** cannot.

bark Bark is also the outside covering of a tree.

barn A barn is a building on a farm where the farmer keeps cows, horses, hay, and grain.

Farmer Grover is going to his **barn** to milk his cows.

basket A basket is a kind of container. You can put things in a basket.

Here is my favorite **basket**— a picnic **basket** filled with apples and bananas and peanut butter sandwiches.

Here is *my* favorite **basket**— a waste**basket.** Just look at all this wonderful crumpled-up paper!

bat A bat is a small, furry animal that flies.

bat A bat is also a wooden stick. You can hit a ball with a bat.

I, the Amazing Mumford, will now pull from this perfectly empty hat two different things with the same name—

A LA PEANUT BUTTER SANDWICHES!

A baseball **bat** and a flying **bat.**

bath   When you take a bath, you wash all over.

bathtub   A bathtub is a thing in which you take a bath.

Ernie and Rubber Duckie are taking a **bath** in the **bathtub.**

be   To be is to live or exist.

I will plant these seeds, and soon there will **be** carrots growing here.

CARROT SEEDS

be   Sometimes we use the word be to tell someone how to act.

Be careful not to step on my seeds!

beach   A beach is the sandy or pebbly land next to an ocean, a lake, or a river.

Ernie and Bert are at the **beach.**

bean   A bean is a vegetable.

Here are some **beans.** They are all delicious.

string bean

kidney bean

lima bean

A jelly**bean** is not a vegetable. It is a piece of candy shaped like a **bean.**

jellybean

bear A bear is a big, furry animal.

Once upon a time there were three **bears**—

beautiful When something you see or hear pleases you very much, you say it is beautiful.

Oh, what **beautiful** flowers!

because Because is a word that tells why.

I am the Count. Do you know why they call me the Count? **Because** I love to count things.

1, 2, 3... three **bears**! Wonderful!

bed A bed is a place to sleep.

Someone is sleeping in my **bed**!

bee A bee is a flying insect that buzzes. Some bees sting.

Bees love flowers. So do I. But I do not love **bees**.

before Before is a word that means earlier than.

This is the chair **before** Herry Monster sat in it.

This is the chair after Herry Monster sat in it.

begin When you begin, you start.

I **begin** each day by washing my face.

beginning The beginning is the start of something.

Prairie Dawn always gets excited at the **beginning** of her favorite TV show.

behind When you are behind something, you are in back of it.

Farley is sitting **behind** Prairie Dawn. He wishes he were in front of her.

believe When you believe something, you think it is true.

Mr. Snuffle-upagus is real. But nobody believes me.

I believe you, Bird.

belong When something belongs to you, you own it.

Rubber Duckie **belongs** to Ernie.

belong When something belongs, it is in the right place.

Hey, Bert. Three of these things belong together. One of these things is not the same.

That's right, Ernie. That sock is a piece of clothing. The other things are toys. They belong in your toy box! What are they doing in my laundry basket?

bell A bell is something that rings.

Roosevelt Franklin is ringing his bicycle **bell**.

RING A LING

DING DONG

Cookie Monster is ringing a door**bell**.

below
When you are below something, you are lower than it is.

I, Grover, am flying my little airplane **below** the clouds. Hello, up there, little cloud!

beside When you are beside something, you are next to it.

Herry Monster is standing **beside** the Busby twins.

between When you are between two things, you are in the space that separates them.

Herry Monster is standing **between** the Busby twins.

bicycle A bicycle is a machine that people ride. It has two wheels, handlebars, and pedals to make the wheels go around.

Grover likes to ride his **bicycle.**

Another name for a **bicycle** is bike.

big Something big needs more room than something little. It is large, not small.

Big Bird needs a **big** nest.

Little Bird needs a little nest.

bird A bird is an animal with feathers and a beak. Most birds can fly.

Big **Bird**'s feathers are yellow.

Big Bird's Bird Guide

Backyard Birds

robin

bluejay

cardinal

Barnyard Birds

turkey

chicken

duck

Big and Little Birds

hummingbird

ostrich

Plain and Fancy Birds

peacock

pigeon

Noisy and Quiet Birds

swan

woodpecker

birthday   Your birthday is the day of the year when you were born.

HAPPY BIRTHDAY BIG BIRD

BIRD-SEED

Gadzooks! What have we here? **Birthday** presents? **Birthday** cake? A banner that says HAPPY **BIRTHDAY**, BIG BIRD? I wonder what this means. I, Sherlock Hemlock, the world's greatest detective, will solve the mystery.

Hi, Sherlock! Isn't this a nice **birthday** party for Big Bird?

Aha! I have it! This is a **birthday** party for Big Bird!

bite   When you take a bite of something, you break off a piece with your teeth.

Egad! Someone has taken a **bite** out of the birthday cake! Who could it be?

block   A block is a building toy.

I, the Amazing Mumford, will now pull from this perfectly empty hat two different things with the same name.

A LA PEANUT BUTTER SANDWICHES!

block   A block is also a place for buildings in a town or city. Your block is your street from one corner to the other.

You see? Here is one toy building **block**! But where is that other kind of **block**?

You are standing on it, Mumphie!

blood   Blood is the red liquid that is pumped to all parts of your body by your heart. Blood flows through tubes called veins and arteries.

Here is a picture that shows how **blood** flows through your body.

blow   When you blow, air comes out of your mouth.

Here is something
to **blow** on.

Here is something
to **blow** up.

Here is something
to **blow** away.

Here is something
to **blow** out.

board   A board is a flat piece of wood.

Bert has some **boards.**
He is going to build a birdhouse.

NAILS

boat   A boat is something that floats in the water and can carry people and things.

Some **boats** have sails.

Some **boats** have engines.

Some **boats** have oars.

Some **boats**
have leaks.

body   Your body is all of you, from the top of your head to the tips of your toes.

Can you name the parts of Bert's **body**?

hair
forehead
head
cheek
eyebrow
eye
ear
mouth
chin
shoulder
nose
neck
chest
back
arm
stomach
hip
bellybutton
wrist
hand
elbow
finger
knee
leg
ankle
toe
foot

bones A bone is a part of your body. Your bones are hard. Look up the word skeleton.

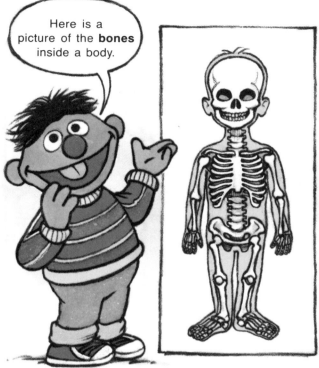

Here is a picture of the **bones** inside a body.

book A book has sheets of paper between two covers. Most books have words. Some books have pictures.

This dictionary is a **book.**

boot A boot is a shoe that covers the ankle.

Ernie is wearing red rain **boots** over his shoes.

Rodeo Rosie is wearing cowgirl **boots** instead of shoes.

born When a baby has grown big enough to be outside its mother's body, it is ready to be born.

This calf was just **born.**

both Both means two together.

Both Biff and Sully are eating lunch.

bottle A bottle is a kind of container, usually made of glass or plastic. A bottle can hold something that you pour.

Sully, pass me that **bottle** of Figgy Fizz, please.

bottom   The bottom is the place farthest from the top.

Hey, Bert, old buddy, can I look at one of your bottle caps?

Sure, Ernie.

What did you do that for, Ernie?

I wanted to see the one on the **bottom.**

bow   A bow is a fancy knot. When you tie a bow, you make a knot with loops.

bow   A bow is also a special kind of stick. It is used to play many stringed instruments.

I, the Amazing Mumford, will now pull from this perfectly empty hat two different things with the same name.

A LA PEANUT BUTTER SANDWICHES!

One beautiful ribbon **bow** and one violin **bow!**

bowl   A bowl is a deep, round dish.

What kind of cereal does a ghost put in his cereal **bowl?**

Ghost Toasties!

box   A box is a kind of container. You can put things in a box.

Gee, Bert, I didn't know oatmeal came in so many different kinds of **boxes.**

boy   A boy is a child who will grow up to be a man.

I am a **boy.** My father is a man. When I grow up, I will be a man, too.

bread Bread is something to eat. It is made from flour and baked in an oven.

Three of these things belong together. One of these things is not the same.

The clock does not belong. You cannot eat a clock. But you can eat loaves of **bread.**

white bread

French bread

rye bread

clock

break When something breaks, it falls to pieces or stops working.

Oops! I did not mean to **break** the vase.

Ernie, stop playing with the television set or you'll **break** it. Then I won't be able to watch the Pigeon News.

breakfast Breakfast is the meal that you eat in the morning.

Bert has oatmeal for **breakfast** every day.

bridge A bridge is something that is built across water, roads, or deep valleys. People, cars, and other things can cross over a bridge.

The Count is driving his bat car over the **bridge.**

bring When you bring something, you have it with you when you come.

Big Bird, you didn't have to **bring** me a present.

I **brought** you a new vase.

broom A broom is a special kind of brush on the end of a long stick. It is used to sweep up dirt and trash.

Uh-oh! Herry Monster broke the new vase. Big Bird is using a **broom** to sweep up the pieces.

brother If your mother and father have another child who is a boy, he is your brother.

He is my **brother.**

She is my sister.

brush A brush is a tool made of bristles fastened to a handle.

Biff wants to paint the hallway. He has a can of paint. Which **brush** is better for Biff?

paint brush

tooth brush

PAINT

Sully wants to clean his teeth. He has some toothpaste. Which **brush** is better for Sully?

build When you build, you put pieces together to make something.

Bert is going to **build** a birdhouse.

NAILS

Bert is **building** the birdhouse.

building A building is a place with walls and a roof.

Here is the **building** that Bert built. It is for the birds.

bump When you bump into something, you hit it with your body—usually by mistake.

bump A bump is a lump.

Watch out, Bert! You will **bump** your head.

Bert **bumped** into the birdhouse.

Now Bert has a **bump** on his head.

burn When something catches on fire, it burns. It gives out light and heat.

My candle has started to **burn**. Now I can see to count my pictures. But first, let me count my candle. 1… one candle!

Some things turn to ashes when they **burn**.

bus A bus is something that you ride in. It has lots of seats. A bus can carry many people from place to place.

Here comes the **bus**!

Five people are waiting at the **bus** stop.

busy When you are busy, you have lots to do.

The bird watcher is **busy** watching birds.

The builder is **busy** building a building.

The bus driver is **busy** driving a bus.

SESAME STREET

NEW BUILDING GOING UP HERE!

The bricklayer is **busy** laying bricks.

but But means except.

Everyone is busy **but** Big Bird.

I feel like reading, **but** I don't have a book.

CAB

butcher A butcher is someone who cuts and sells meat for people to cook.

BUTCHER SHOP

Herry Monster went to the **butcher** shop. He bought some meat from the **butcher**.

butterfly A butterfly is an insect with a thin body and four wings.

Catching a **butterfly** is not easy.

button A button is small and flat and usually round. Some buttons hold clothes together. Some buttons make things work.

Hey, Ernie, look at all the different **buttons** in my **button** collection.

Gee, Bert, you are missing the best **button** of all.

Which one is that?

The belly**button**. Heh! Heh!

Grover the elevator operator is pushing the **button** for the tenth floor.

Going up?

10 9 8 7 6 5 4 3 2 1

buy When you buy something, you pay for it. After you buy something, it belongs to you.

Hey, you. How'd ya like to **buy** this terrific letter B? Lots of words begin with the letter B. Even *begin* begins with the letter B.

B

by By means near or beside.

Oscar's garbage can is the one **by** the steps.

GO AWAY!

by If something was done by you, you did it.

I painted this picture all **by** myself.

By Big Bird

These are supposed to be the B words, but I can't even find some of my favorite words that begin with B—words like bellyache, bothersome, blecch, and BEAT IT!

Big Bird's **B** Rebus

...Bert

...bed

...balloon

...basket

....buttons

.....broom

....bath

A rebus
is a story
that uses pictures
in place of words.
Here are the pictures
I have used in
my **B** rebus.

...boat

...bottle

...banana

....bottle cap

...box

Bert's Day in Bed

One day [Bert] felt bad, so he decided to stay in [bed]. Ernie brought [Bert] a big [balloon] to cheer him up. But [Bert] still felt bad. So Ernie brought [Bert] a [basket] of [buttons]. But [Bert] still felt bad. Then Ernie brought [Bert] his favorite [broom]. But [Bert] just said," Go away."

"I know," said Ernie," what you need is to take a [bath] and play with your toy [boat]."

"Don't bother me," said .
While Ernie was thinking how to
cheer up , he brought out a
of soda and opened it.
The fell on the .
"Wow!" said . "This is the
most beautiful I've ever
seen. I feel much better."
And he jumped out of
and put the in his
special .

A and **B** Riddles

What question can you
ask that can never
be answered yes?

Are you asleep?

What has a bark but
cannot bite?

A tree!